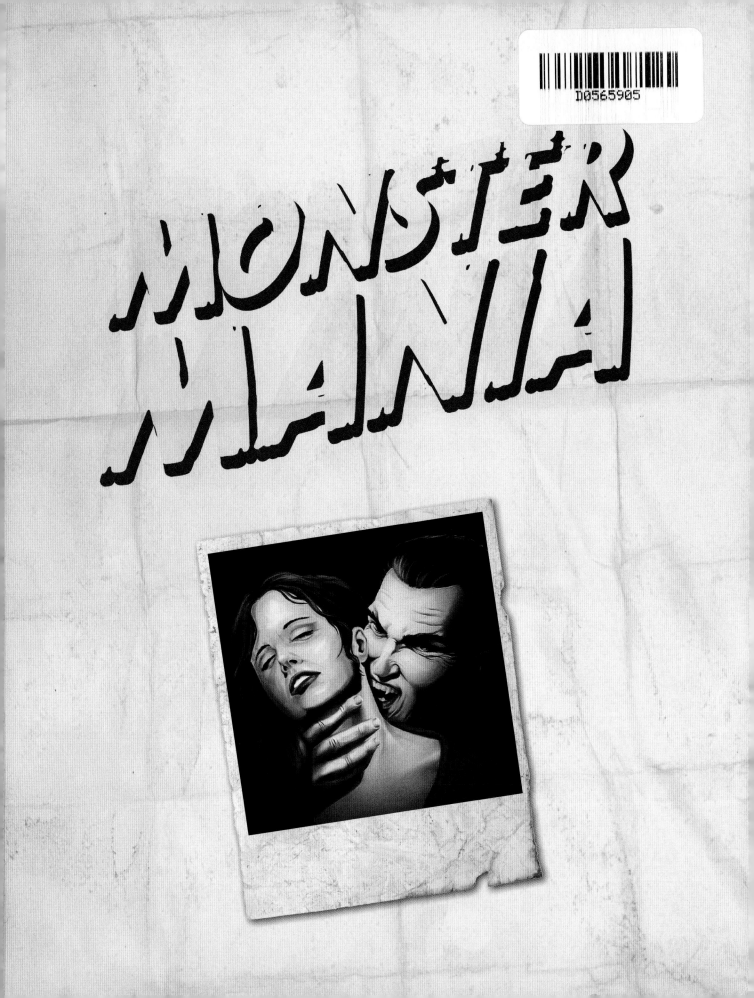

Printed in Guangdong, China
10 9 8 7 6 5 4 3 2 1

Illustrator: Vincent Boulanger
Editor: Amanda Askew
Designer: Matthew Kelly
Picture Researcher: Maria Joannou

Words in **bold** can be found in the Glossary on page 93.

Acknowledgements

Alamy Images Photos 12/Archives du 7eme Art 14, Mary Evans Picture Library 58, 74, Johner Images 54r, The Marsden Archive 83b, Universal Images Group Limited 31r, Photos 12/Archives du 7eme Art 55b, 57b, 64, Pictorial Press Ltd 36, 92; **Bridgeman Art Library** Private Collection 66, Kharbine-Tapabor, Paris, France 59t; **Corbis** Images.com 11, Bruno Ehrs 47r, Jessica Rinaldi/Reuters 82, 91t; **DK Images** Steve Gorton 19 **Getty Images** Hulton Archive/Stringer 34b, The Bridgeman Art Library 35b, Workbook Stock/Luca Zampedri 67, Stone/Ralf Nau 70, National Geographic/Steve And Donna O'Meara 71b, Jane Sweeney/Robert Harding 78, Hulton Archive/Mills 79b, Time & Life Pictures 83t; **Istockphoto** FotografiaBasica 43b, Mediadeva 47l, David Naylor 54; René Mansi 54l, Ideeone 63b; **Photolibrary** AlaskaStock 23l, Superstock 62; **Photoshot** Universal Pictures/Starstock 27b; **Rex Features** Universal/Everett15, Everett Collection 18, SNAP 38, 50; **Science Photo Library** Garion Hutchings 87b; **Shutterstock** Gian Corrêa Saléro 42, Elixirpix 71t, Stephen B. Goodwin 43t, Csaba Peterdi 46, Olly 75, Olemac 21b, Rickshu 22r, R. Formidable 79t , Craig Dingle 51b, Petr Pilar 55t, Martin Muránsky 30, Wheatley 31l, Marcelo Dufflocq W. 34t, Steve Mann 35t, Nikola Bilic 63tl, Flashgun 63tr, Hannah Eckman 63c (bullets), 63c (garlic) Dariusz Majgier; **Topham Picturepoint** 27t, Fortean/Sibbick 39, Anthony Wallis/Fortean Picture Library 19b The Granger Collection 51t, Fortean 86, 87t, AP 90, Charles Walker 91b.

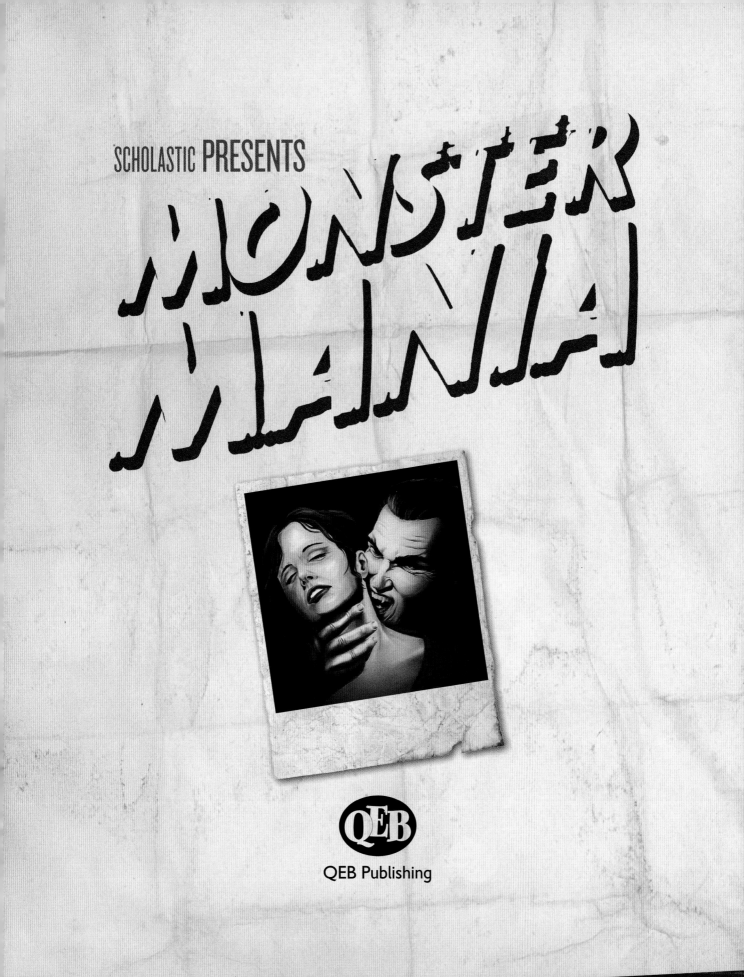

CONTENTS

Werewolves

Vampires

Ghosts

WEREWOLVES

A WORLD OF WEREWOLVES

According to old **folk stories**, werewolves are human beings who change their shape into wolflike creatures. They become savage monsters that hunt, attack, bite, and kill. But no one is sure whether they really exist.

Werewolves are creatures of the night, but as the darkness fades away and daylight returns, they shift their shapes back into human form. Werewolves lead double lives, hiding inside their human hosts.

But, when werewolf attacks are suspected, panic sets in. Long ago, in parts of Europe, hunters tracked down werewolves, trials were held, and people thought to be these monsters were put to death.

Meaning of werewolf

The word "werewolf" is made from the Old English word "wer," which means "man," added to the word "wolf." It literally means "man-wolf."

A scratch from a werewolf was said to be enough to cause a person to change from human to wolf.

WHO'S WHO
AMONG WEREWOLVES?

FAIRYTALE WEREWOLVES

In fairy tales there is sometimes a creature described as a "big bad wolf." For example, in the well-known tale of *Little Red Riding Hood*, an old woman disappears and a wicked wolf takes her place. In other words, the old woman has shape-shifted from a human into a wolf, and that means she is a werewolf.

AND THE REST...

VOLUNTARY WEREWOLVES

Voluntary werewolves are people who actually want to become werewolves. They are the opposite of **involuntary** werewolves.

IMAGINARY WEREWOLVES

These are people who think they are werewolves. The truth is they are ordinary humans with vivid imaginations.

INVOLUNTARY WEREWOLVES

Involuntary werewolves are people who never set out to become werewolves. Something happened to them and they changed into monsters.

11

The Very First
WEREWOLF

It's hard to be certain where werewolves came from, but one of the first stories was told by the people of ancient Greece about 2,500 years ago.

There was once a king called Lycaon (say: *lie-kay-on*) who ruled over Arcadia, a region of Greece. He was not a religious man, and this made the gods angry. Zeus, the king of the gods, decided to visit Lycaon to find out what sort of a person he was.

Zeus disguised himself as a peasant and asked Lycaon for food and shelter. Lycaon had a feeling he was being tricked. A banquet was prepared, but instead of feeding his guest with animal meat, Lycaon served him human flesh. If the stranger was indeed a god, he would be disgusted by such vile meat.

The great god Zeus came down to Earth to discover if King Lycaon was a good or a bad person.

Werewolf for nine years

There is another version of this story. It says that every time a sacrifice was made at Lycaon's altar, a man was turned into a wolf. After nine years, the werewolf changed back into human form—but only if it had not eaten human flesh. If it had tasted human meat, it would remain a werewolf forever.

When Zeus saw the food, he knew that Lycaon was indeed a bad person. He threw the table over and hurled bolts of lightning at Lycaon's sons, killing them all, except one.

Zeus hurled his lightning bolts with deadly accuracy.

As for Lycaon, Zeus dealt him a punishment far worse than death. He turned him into a wolf, for only a wolf would enjoy the taste of human flesh.

Werewolves are lycanthropes

A werewolf can also be called a **lycanthrope**. This comes from two Greek words—*lykos* meaning "wolf," and *anthropos* meaning "human."

Lycaon's fate was sealed, and he became the first werewolf.

13

How WEREWOLVES Are Made

According to stories, there are two ways for a human to become a werewolf. The person either wants to change into a werewolf, or the person is a victim and tries to resist—but he or she cannot stop the shape-shifting process.

I WANT TO BE A WEREWOLF

People who want to be werewolves are voluntary werewolves. They rub ointment made from herbs on their bodies, chant spells, tie belts of wolfskin around their waist, and cover themselves with wolf pelts. Some werewolves claim to have been transformed by sipping water from the pawprint of a wolf, or by sleeping in a wolf's lair. These people think they have been transformed, and for a time they act as if they are wolves.

The human body changes to one covered in thick fur, with wolflike claws and teeth.

I DON'T WANT TO BE A WEREWOLF

People who do not want to be werewolves are involuntary werewolves. Legend has it that for them, it might start with a scratch or a bite from a werewolf, and when this happens, their fate is sealed. In some stories, a person becomes a werewolf when a sorcerer curses him or her, or a magician casts a spell on them.

Once the process of **transformation** from human to werewolf begins, nothing can stop it (*An American Werewolf in London, 1981*).

The wolf belt

Many old stories, especially ones from northern Europe, talk about **wolf belts**. Made from strips of wolfskin, they were said to work like lucky charms. Wearing a wolf belt made a person feel like he or she had a wolf's strength.

15

Little Red RIDING HOOD

Once upon a time, there was a little girl who lived near a forest. Whenever she went out, she wore a bright-red riding cloak, so people called her Little Red Riding Hood.

One day, she set out to visit her grandmother, whose cottage was among the trees. On the way she met a wolf, who asked her where she was going. No sooner had she replied, than the wolf ran away.

The wolf went to the grandmother's house and knocked on the door. Thinking it was Little Red Riding Hood, the old lady opened the door—and the wolf leapt upon her and gobbled her up. The wolf got dressed in the grandmother's clothes and climbed into her bed.

Little Red Riding Hood was shocked to see the wolf.

When Little Red Riding Hood arrived, she said,

"What big ears you have!"

"All the better to hear you with, my dear," replied the wolf.

"What big teeth you have!" said Little Red Riding Hood.

"All the better to eat you with!" roared the wolf, jumping onto Little Red Riding Hood and swallowing her up.

Big bad wolf

Wolves are the baddies in many fairy tales. In *The Wolf and the Seven Young Kids*, a hungry wolf eats seven baby goats, which are eventually set free unharmed. In *The Three Little Pigs*, a wolf is killed by a pig, but not until the wolf has tried to eat the pigs.

The hunter set Little Red Riding Hood and her grandmother free.

A short while later, a hunter passed by and saw the wolf. He knew it must have eaten the old lady, so the hunter took a pair of scissors and cut open the wolf's belly. Out climbed Little Red Riding Hood and her grandmother. Then they packed stones into the wolf's body and sewed up the cut. When the wolf woke, it was so heavy it could hardly move, and it dropped down dead.

How to Spot a
WEREWOLF

Stories say that werewolves lead double lives. In the daytime they appear in their human form, but at night they are transformed into savage beasts.

A WEREWOLF IN HUMAN FORM

At first sight, a werewolf in its unchanged form looks like a normal human. But if the person seems nervous or restless, then a werewolf might be lurking inside.

Other important clues are said to be eyebrows that come together on the bridge of the nose; long, curved fingernails; and canine or biting teeth that seem long and sharp, more like a big dog's or a wolf's than a human's.

There can be no doubt that this is the face of a werewolf, not a human.

Sign of the werewolf

According to stories, werewolves are marked with a five-pointed star, or **pentagram**, usually on their chest or hand. It's always there, and when they are in their human form they cover it up.

If the person is cut, fur might be seen within the wound. Bristles might be spotted under the tongue, and beware of people who have fur on the palms of their hands. None of these features is right for a human, so it must mean there is an animal hiding inside the person.

Human fingers are transformed into animal claws.

A WEREWOLF IN WEREWOLF FORM

A fully transformed werewolf doesn't look anything like a wolf. It is bigger, and while an ordinary wolf has a tail, a werewolf never does. It walks upright on two legs, not on all fours. Its eyes are fiery red and its fur has a silvery sheen. If the creature speaks with a human voice, then it can only be a werewolf.

A werewolf always walks on two legs, rather than four like a wolf.

You are a werewolf!

The biggest clue of all to spotting a werewolf is this: an injury to a werewolf will show up in exactly the same place on its human body. So, if a werewolf is cut on the left leg, there will be an identical cut in the same place on its human leg.

19

An American
WEREWOLF

P eople from Europe who settled in North America took werewolf stories with them, and soon America had its own stories of man-wolves.

This story comes from **Pennsylvania**

Snydertown is a small town in Pennsylvania. The townsfolk became suspicious of an old man who lived on his own and didn't mix with other people. He was often seen visiting the farm of Mr. and Mrs. Paul, watching their daughter, May, as she looked after the family's sheep.

The creepy old man watched May Paul as she tended to the sheep.

Although there were many wolves in the area, and sheep were often attacked by them, whenever the old man showed up, the wolves kept away. A rumor started that he was a werewolf.

The hunter shot the wolf, soon to be discovered as the old man.

One night, when the Moon was full, a hunter saw a wolf on the prowl. Thinking it was out to kill sheep, he took aim with his rifle. The wolf let out a mighty howl as the hunter's bullet ripped through its body. The beast was injured and managed to run away, leaving a trail of blood for the hunter to follow.

The hunter tracked it to a hut, and instead of a wolf, he found the body of the old man, dead from a bullet wound. There could be no doubt that the man had indeed been a shape-shifter.

The Beast of Bray Road

A more recent story about an American werewolf comes from Wisconsin. Sightings of a tall, wolflike creature have been reported near the town of Elkhorn, along a quiet country road. The Beast of Bray Road, as it's called, has been seen many times over the years.

21

HOWLING AT THE MOON

Since ancient times the Moon has been linked to strange events on Earth. When there's a full moon in the sky, it's werewolf night. According to folktales, it's the Moon that brings these shape-shifters out, changing humans into howling monsters.

The changing shape of the Moon has become linked with the transformation of man into monster.

As a full moon rises, a werewolf emerges, ready to rampage through the night.

CHANGING SHAPE

The Moon seems to change its shape throughout the month, from a crescent to a full circle, and then fading from sight. Werewolves are said to break out of their human body during a full moon—its power is so great it pulls the beast from its human host.

MOONLIGHT

In the past, it was thought moonlight changed people into "lunatics," which comes from *luna*, the Latin word for "moon." Even the British government believed this, and in 1842 a law was made that said people who suffered from "Moon madness'" acted strangely when the Moon was full.

Moon power

It's not just werewolves that come out on a moonlit night. Folktales are full of witches and fairies who are at their most active when the Moon is full, and ugly hags are transformed into beautiful maidens.

In this Victorian illustration, a werewolf pounces on a man during the light of a full moon.

Wolves are more active on bright, moonlit nights than on dark, moonless nights.

HOWLING AT THE MOON

Werewolves and ordinary wolves are said to howl at the Moon, as if moonlight sets something off inside them. In werewolf stories, the Moon is usually a vital part of the plot, causing the transformation process to start and the howling to begin.

Peter Stubbe, WEREWOLF OF BEDBURG

Around 400 years ago, rumors were started about a man from Bedburg, Germany, who believed he was a werewolf. This caused panic, and local people lived in fear.

The man's name was Peter Stubbe, and he was a farmer with a secret. One day, a young boy was snatched by a wolf, and when it was tracked to its lair, the hunters saw it shape-shift into human form. At that point they knew they were dealing with a werewolf—none other than Farmer Stubbe.

Hunters saw the boy had been taken by a werewolf.

Stubbe was arrested and sent to trial. He confessed to having a wolf belt. Whenever he tied it around his waist, he changed into a savage beast with cruel teeth, fire-red eyes, and paws for hands. He would search out anyone who had ever upset him and tear them to pieces.

Stubbe was a voluntary werewolf—someone who wanted to change into a monster.

Cannibal werewolves

Peter Stubbe said he had eaten parts of his victims' bodies, which meant he was a **cannibal**. Werewolves are often described as cannibals. Perhaps this is why werewolves have the strength of many people.

The Werewolf of Bedburg, as Peter Stubbe became known, was sentenced to death. He met a particularly grisly end in October 1589, involving painful stretching, before his head was cut off and his body burned.

25

Powers of
WEREWOLVES

Werewolves are said to be powerful creatures. Their power is everything—without it they would be as weak as when they are human.

STRENGTH AND POWER

Stories about werewolves say that these part-human, part-animal beings have the strength of many ordinary humans. Some people think this strength comes from werewolves eating their victims. The more they eat, the stronger they get.

In pictures, artists make werewolves look as strong as possible.

Wolf sense

A werewolf has the intelligence of a human. This means it can track and recognize its victims and avoid any traps that might have been set for it.

SUPER SENSES

Werewolves are creatures of the night, with excellent powers of seeing in the dark. They also have a good sense of smell. These two senses give the monster a huge advantage over their human victims. Werewolves can easily detect humans in the dark, whereas human sight and smell will not pick up the danger until it is too late to escape.

Its keen senses of sight and smell help a werewolf to detect a victim at night.

CHANGING SHAPE

Werewolves are said to have the power to change their shape from human to beast, and then back again. Each time this happens, new body tissue is formed, and there are some who say this gives werewolves the power to live forever.

Powerful jaws packed with sharp, biting teeth can easily tear through flesh.

Werewolves OF GREIFSWALD

This story was retold in a book by Jodocus Temme, who came across it in northeast Germany. It tells of a time when werewolves plagued the old, historic town of Greifswald.

Greifswald is an old town, with one of the oldest universities in Europe. It was said that werewolves had taken up residence in the center of town and any student who dared to walk the streets after dark would be set upon by the monsters.

The citizens of Greifswald were under attack from werewolves.

Wanting to fight back, one of the students had an idea. He suggested that they should collect as much silver as they could. Buttons, buckles, goblets, jewelry, forks, and spoons were gathered and thrown into a furnace, where they were turned into liquid silver. Carefully, the liquid was molded into small balls of silver.

The students fought back, and their silver bullets destroyed the werewolves.

This story comes from
GERMANY

The students entered the dark streets, and the werewolves attacked. Raising their **muskets** and pistols, the young men aimed at the beasts and fired. Their silver bullets tore into the werewolves, killing every last one.

Protection from
WEREWOLVES

Werewolves are described in stories as tough creatures without any fear. Once they've moved into an area, there's very little that can be done to keep them away.

STAY INDOORS

The best protection is to never go outside when it is a full moon and stay well away from forests where werewolves might lurk.

ODD BEHAVIOR

Anyone could be a werewolf in disguise. Nervous, fidgety behavior, unexplained cuts and bruises, and a constant thirst are all signs of a possible shape-shifter, and the person should be avoided, especially at full moon.

It was thought that silver was protection against werewolves. People kept silver objects in their homes and carried silver coins with them.

PRAYING TO THE GODS

Prayers were offered to Diana, the ancient goddess of wild animals and the Moon. Her magic was thought to keep werewolves away. People also prayed to St. Hubert, the patron saint of hunting. It was believed he could cure rabies, a deadly disease that passed to humans from wolves and dogs. If St. Hubert could do this, then perhaps he could also offer protection from werewolves.

People prayed to Diana, goddess of the Moon, for protection against werewolves.

Superstitious people grew wolfsbane in their gardens. This plant was believed to repel (banish) wolves.

CASTING SPELLS

Spells were also said, and whoever cast the spell dripped oil into a candle flame to make the magic work.

Werewolf cures

In parts of Germany, it was said that a werewolf could be cured if it was called three times by its human name. In Denmark, shouting at a werewolf, as if it was nothing more than a big bad dog, was thought to turn it back into its human form.

31

Jean Grenier, A TEENAGE WEREWOLF

Jean Grenier, a teenage boy from France, was almost put to death in 1603 because he believed he was a werewolf.

In the courtroom, 14-year-old Jean told the most amazing tale. Three years before, he had met the Master of the Forest. This evil being scratched Jean, then gave him magic ointment for his skin and a wolfskin cloak. When he wore the cloak, he was transformed into a werewolf.

Dressed in wolfskin, Jean Grenier imagined he was a werewolf.

Jean was neither shy nor embarrassed by what he said he had done. As a werewolf he had frightened people, some of whom he claimed to have attacked and eaten. The boy was found guilty and was sentenced to be hanged.

The judge pronounced the death sentence on the teenager who claimed to be a werewolf.

It's all in the mind

Johann Weyer (c.1515–1588), a doctor from the Netherlands, was one of the first people to ask if werewolves were real or not. He said they came from people's imaginations. It was a long time before his idea was accepted.

While Jean was in prison awaiting his fate, his case was looked at in more detail. It turned out that no one had been reported missing, and no victims of wolf attacks had been found. The court decided that Jean Grenier had made everything up, looking for attention. He was sent to a monastery, where he spent the rest of his life.

How to Slay a WEREWOLF

For those who believed in werewolves, the ultimate challenge was knowing how to destroy them. The first task was always to identify the werewolf, which was difficult when the werewolf was in its human form.

DESTROYING THE HUMAN FORM

In the past, once a person was arrested on suspicion of being a werewolf, they were forced to confess their crimes, often under painful torture.

Their bodies were searched for clues, such as a cut in the same place where a wolf had been injured. Some were sent for trial, and most were found guilty. The punishment was death, either by beheading or burning at the stake.

People accused of being werewolves were put to death.

34

DESTROYING THE WEREWOLF FORM

There is only one way to slay a werewolf in its monster form—shooting it with a silver bullet. This precious metal was believed to have a power that could defeat evil.

People thought that as soon as a silver bullet burst into a werewolf's body, the creature would die, killing its human form, too.

In folk stories, the only sure way of destroying a werewolf is by shooting it with silver bullets—no other metal will do.

The Beast of Gévaudan

In 1764, a monstrous wolf terrorized the region of Gévaudan, France. Many people thought it was a werewolf. A local farmer, Jean Chastel, killed the Beast of Gévaudan with silver bullets. This may be where the idea of killing werewolves with silver bullets comes from.

TIMELINE

1000S The word "werewulf" was first written down in English.

1039-1101 Life of Vseslav of Polotsk, a Russian prince described in folk stories as a werewolf.

1490S Trials were held in Switzerland of women accused of riding wolves.

1520-1630 In France, as many as 30,000 people were accused of being werewolves.

1521 Three men from Poligny, France, were found guilty of being werewolves and were burned at the stake.

1525-1589 Life of Peter Stubbe, who was found guilty of being a werewolf and was executed.

1603 Jean Grenier, a teenage boy from France, claimed he was a werewolf.

1640S A pack of werewolves was said to have plagued the town of Greifswald, Germany.

1697 The folk story *Little Red Riding Hood* was first written down.

1764 A large wolf, thought by some people to be a werewolf, terrorized the region of Gévaudan, France.

1913 The first werewolf movie was made, called *The Werewolf*. It was 18 minutes long and was a silent movie.

1941 *The Wolf Man* was released, one of the most famous werewolf movies ever made.

1981 Two famous werewolf movies came out, *The Howling* and *An American Werewolf in London*.

An American Werewolf in London is a popular comedy horror about two friends and their encounter with werewolves.

PolyGram Pictures presents a Lycanthrope Films Limited production
An American Werewolf in London
starring David Naughton, Jenny Agutter, Griffin Dunne & John Woodvine
Original music by Elmer Bernstein · Executive producers Peter Guber & Jon Peter
Produced by George Folsey, Jr. · Written and directed by John Landis
PolyGram Pictures   "Meco's Impressions of An American Werewolf in London"
Marketed by PolyGram Records

1989 The first sighting of a wolflike creature known as the Beast of Bray Road, in Wisconsin.

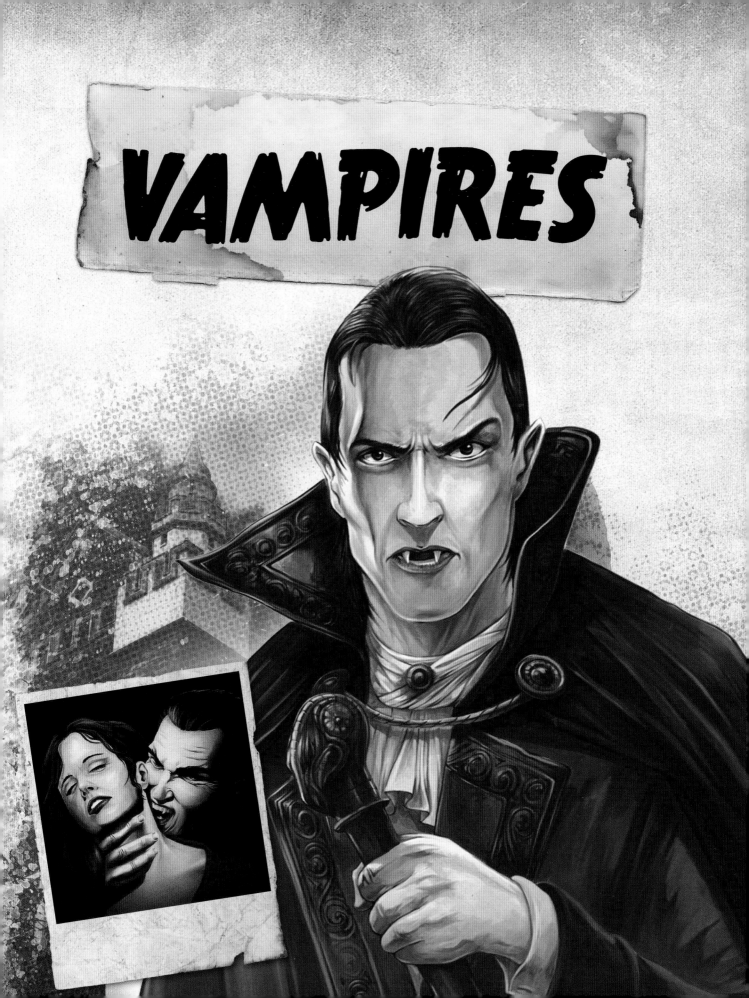

A World of VAMPIRES

Who or what are vampires? From folk stories and accounts by investigators, it's clear that vampires are monstrous creatures—the **undead**.

Legend has it vampires have survived death and have come back to prey on the living. They need food—blood. Sucking the blood of humans and animals, they leave their victims dead or barely alive.

Count Dracula is the world's most famous vampire. Here, he is played by Christopher Lee (Dracula, 1958) and is shown drinking the blood from one of his many victims.

The meaning of "vampire"

No one really knows where the word "vampire" comes from. Some people say it comes from the Lithuanian word wempti, which means "to drink." Some say it's from the Turkish word uber, meaning "witch."

Vampires are hunters of the night and return to their resting places before the first light of day. They are feared by all and hunted by a brave few who have done all they can to destroy them, before they can spread vampirism any farther. But no one knows for sure whether vampires ever existed.

WHO'S WHO AMONG VAMPIRES?

ANIMAL VAMPIRES

These supernatural creatures attack their prey and drink their blood. The chupacabra, or goat-sucker, of Puerto Rico and Mexico is a famous example.

Chupacabra comes from the Spanish words, *chupar*, meaning "to suck," and *cabra*, meaning "goat"—together, they make goat-sucker. Eyewitnesses claim that many livestock, especially goats, have been attacked and their blood drained.

AND THE REST...

LIVING VAMPIRES

Real people who call themselves vampires, such as Countess Elizabeth Bathory (1560–1614), who bathed in blood.

SPIRIT VAMPIRES

Vampires that exist without physical bodies. They can float, fly, appear, and disappear, and can change their shape at will.

UNDEAD VAMPIRES

Vampires that were humans. They were attacked by vampires and have been transformed into undead creatures.

DRACULA, PRINCE OF DARKNESS

When Jonathan Harker, an English solicitor, reached the mountains of **Transylvania**, he entered Count Dracula's castle. Dracula planned to move to England, and Harker was there to help him.

As the days passed, Harker grew concerned about Dracula. Harker saw him only at night, and Dracula never ate or drank. When Harker discovered Dracula sleeping in a coffin in the daytime, he knew he was staring at a vampire.

This story comes from
ENGLAND and TRANSYLVANIA

Dracula's daytime resting place was discovered by Jonathan Harker.

Leaving Harker prisoner in the castle, Dracula boarded a ship for England. In the daytime, he slept in a box filled with soil from his homeland, and at night he bit the sailors and drank their blood. As the ship approached England, it was wrecked in a storm. Dracula escaped.

Now in England, Dracula sucked the blood of a young girl, Lucy Westenra, who became very weak. When Abraham Van Helsing, a vampire hunter, examined her, he discovered that she had been bitten by a vampire. Nothing could be done to save her, and Lucy died.

The search was on to destroy Dracula, who had fled back to Transylvania. Vampire hunters, led by Van Helsing, opened the vampire's coffin and plunged a knife into Dracula's heart, and Jonathan Harker slit the monster's throat. Dracula was dead.

The ship that Dracula traveled to England on, the *Demeter*, ran aground off the coast of Whitby, northeast England.

Dracula, the Book

Dracula is the title of a book written by Irish author Bram Stoker (1847–1912). The book, published in 1897, has become the world's best-known vampire story.

How VAMPIRES Are Made

According to vampire stories, there are several ways in which a person becomes one of the undead. It is called **transformation**, or **turning**.

The best-known method is where the vampire bites its victim, usually on the neck, and drinks the blood. The vampire doesn't take too much blood, or the person will die. Instead, the person is left feeling very weak and under the vampire's control.

The vampire sinks its fangs into the victim's neck and drinks the victim's blood.

Power of the Moon

In folk stories, the Moon is often linked with strange events. If a person was born on the night of a new Moon, or as the Moon changed from a new to a full moon, a person could change from human to vampire.

Long life

A person who became a vampire had cheated death. Instead of living for a short time, like a human, they could live for hundreds of years. They might even be immortal, which means they could live forever.

The vampire returns the next night and drinks more of the victim's blood. Last of all, the vampire bites itself on the wrist. Blood pours from the bite, and the victim drinks it. As soon as the person tastes the blood, he or she is turned into a vampire and leaves his or her human life behind.

In some stories, turning was said to be the result of misfortune and bad luck. For example, eating meat from a sheep killed by a wolf was said to cause vampirism. If a cat jumped over a dead body, or if a shadow passed over it, it was thought the person would come back as a vampire.

People can be turned into vampires even after they have died.

43

Arnold Paole, VAMPIRE OF SERBIA

This is a true story from the 1720s about Arnold Paole, who thought he had been attacked by a vampire.

After the attack, Paole searched for the vampire's grave, dug it up, and destroyed the creature. Then he smeared the vampire's blood on his body and ate soil from its grave. This, he hoped, would save him from any more vampire attacks.

This story comes from
SERBIA

Arnold Paole dug up the vampire's grave to destroy it.

However, a few days later, Paole fell, broke his neck, and died. He was buried, but that wasn't the end of him. Rumors spread around the village that Paole had been seen, alive and well. Then, four villagers died, and people became convinced that Paole had come back as a vampire. His grave was opened....

Instead of finding a rotting body, Paole was well preserved. He seemed to have moved inside his coffin, and there was a trickle of blood from his mouth. Fearful, the villagers drove a stake through his heart, cut off his head, and burned his body to end the misery of his attacks.

Plague of vampires

Three years after Paole died, 17 villagers died suddenly. A girl said she had seen one of them alive some time later. These people had become bloodsuckers after eating meat from cattle said to have been bitten by Paole. Their graves were opened, a **stake** was driven through their hearts, and their bodies were burned.

By destroying Paole's body, villagers hoped to defeat the vampire he had become.

How to Spot a VAMPIRE

Stories about blood-sucking vampires have been told for hundreds of years. They are full of clues to help people figure out if a vampire might be nearby.

IN A GRAVEYARD

Graveyards are often said to be the homes of vampires. They sleep under the ground in the day and emerge at night to go about their thirsty work. Groaning sounds from graves, strange mists, and fallen gravestones are signs that vampires might be nearby. Barking dogs in a graveyard and no birdsong are other warning signs of a vampire in the area.

Vampires are said to rest in peace in graveyards, until darkness falls and they emerge from the ground.

THE VICTIMS

Maybe a person has been bitten but hasn't drunk the vampire's blood yet. The obvious clue is a bite mark on the neck. Other symptoms are exhaustion, loss of appetite, and sudden weight loss. Being scared of garlic can also show that the person might be under a vampire's control.

A bite from a vampire usually has two holes where the fangs break the skin.

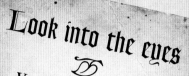

Red eyes, piercing fangs, pale skin—it has to be a vampire.

VAMPIRE BEHAVIOR

According to storytellers, vampires have fangs, stinking breath, long fingernails, a pale complexion, black blood, and hairy palms. They're never seen in the day and will always avoid bright lights at night. They don't eat "normal" food and have powerful senses of smell and hearing. Some vampires can **shape-shift**, transforming themselves into mists or animals, especially bats.

Mercy Brown, VAMPIRE CHILD

Mercy, her mother, and sister were all buried in the Rhode Island cemetery.

Of all the world's vampire stories, this one is one of the strangest. What you are about to read is absolutely true....

George and Mary Brown lived with their three children in a small town in Rhode Island. Mrs. Brown and her daughter, Olive, fell ill with tuberculosis, a lung disease. Nothing could be done and they died. Then another daughter, Mercy, caught the disease and died.

Mr. Brown now feared for Edwin, his son, who was becoming ill. Rumors spread that one of his dead sisters, or even his mother, was a vampire. There was only one way to save Edwin—they had to check the bodies for signs of vampirism.

When the lid on Mercy's coffin was lifted, her body was found to be in good condition. Stranger still, it looked like she had moved. A doctor removed her heart, and it was found to be full of blood. Mercy Brown must have been undead, a vampire!

Her heart was burned and its ashes were mixed with medicine and given to Edwin to drink. Mr. Brown hoped the awful medicine would save Edwin, but it didn't, and the boy died from his illness.

Healthy Heart

Digging up the body of a dead person was often the first step in detecting a vampire. If the heart was healthy and full of blood, it was taken as a sign that the dead person was one of the undead.

Mercy's heart seemed fresh and was full of blood, as if it was somehow still alive.

POWERS OF VAMPIRES

Storytellers have given incredible powers to vampires, which are more than enough to frighten humans.

The key power of a vampire is its ability to live off blood. A vampire isn't a fussy eater and will drink both animal and human blood. It is much more than just food. Blood gives a vampire another of its abilities—the power to live for a long time, maybe even forever.

According to myth, a vampire has power over life and death. If it takes too much blood, the victim dies. But, if it drinks just enough to leave the person helpless, the victim is one step closer to changing into a vampire.

Vampire stories and movies, such as *Nosferatu, the Vampyre* (1979), show how the bloodsuckers drink their victims' blood.

Vampires, unlike humans, have the power of flight, and they can cling to walls and scramble up them, just like many of nature's flying creatures. Wherever they fly to, vampires spread disease.

Vampires have supernatural strength—perhaps they absorb this from their victims, so the more people they kill, the stronger they become. They have the power of mind control, and their human victims fall under their spell.

The Victorians imagined vampires as well-dressed, refined creatures.

Shape-shifters

Vampires can shape-shift at will, changing themselves into animals, especially bats, cats, wolves, dogs, rats, and fleas. They can also become mists and vapors, which allows them to enter victims' houses through gaps around doors and windows.

The Shoemaker VAMPIRE

From Poland comes this sinister tale about a shoemaker transformed into a vampire. The citizens of Wroclau thought a vampire had descended upon them.

It all began on September 20, 1591. An unhappy shoemaker cut his own throat and died. His poor wife covered up the cut, so that no one would know he had taken his own life, and he was laid to rest in the local cemetery.

When people began to say they had seen the shoemaker's ghost, and it had pinched them as they slept, questions were asked. No one felt safe. Finally, the shoemaker's body was dug up.

The townsfolk were afraid to sleep at night, fearing the vampire would pay them a visit.

Are vampires real or not?

In the 1600s and 1700s, there were so many reports of vampires in eastern Europe that the Christian Church decided to investigate. A monk, Dom Augustin Calmet, studied the reports and decided that only superstitious people believed in vampires.

Executed criminals, as well as people thought to be vampires, were buried in unholy ground outside the town.

This story comes from

POLAND

The body was in good condition and hadn't rotted away—a clear sign of vampirism. It was reburied by the town gallows, in **unhallowed** ground. The sightings continued, so the vampire was dug up for a second time, chopped to pieces, and burned until all that was left was ash. The vampire was finally destroyed.

53

Protection From VAMPIRES

There was once a strong belief in vampires, especially in Europe. Many people were so scared by the thought of these vile creatures, they went to great lengths to protect themselves.

A home could be protected by planting thorn bushes around it, such as holly, hawthorn, and wild roses. Their branches were cut off and put against doors and windows, creating a thorny barrier.

Thorny bushes, especially roses and hawthorn, were thought to provide a magical defense against vampires.

Vampires were thought to be fascinated by knots. Some people protected their homes with fishing nets draped in the windows—a vampire would leave them alone because it would have to undo all the knots.

Vampires not welcome

A vampire can enter a house only if it's invited to step inside. However, if the person doesn't know the visitor is a vampire, then it's easy for the monster to trick its way inside.

Garlic was thought to offer protection from vampires, who are said to hate its smell. Crushed garlic was smeared around doors and windows. Garlic bulbs were strung up around the house, worn as necklaces, or just tucked into a pocket.

Strings of garlic bulbs were placed around the house, indoors and outdoors, because vampires dislike the strong smell.

Seed power

One trick was to spread thousands of seeds or handfuls of sand onto the floor. Vampires were obsessed with counting, so they would stop to count the masses of tiny specks. They would still be counting as the sun started to rise, at which point they would retreat to their lair.

Vampires have strong senses. Bright candles were kept burning in homes to keep vampires away. The sound of ringing bells offered protection as vampires hated the noise. They also had a fear of crosses, which were painted on doors with tar. Its strong smell kept vampires well away.

A hunter holds up a cross to Count Dracula (played here by Christopher Lee in Dracula, 1958). Vampires fear the cross.

El Chupacabra
VAMPIRE
GOAT-KILLER

The first eyewitness reports of strange creatures were made in the 1540s, when hundreds of animals were drained of blood.

A group of Spaniards was moving a herd of cattle. They set up camp one evening and during the night 1,500 cattle were killed.

About 400 years later, farmers on the island of Puerto Rico spoke about a creature they called El Chupacabra, which means "the goat-sucker."

In the still of the night, a mysterious blood-sucking creature destroyed hundreds of cattle.

The creature was biting their animals, especially goats, and drinking their blood. The creature was covered in fur, with batlike wings, staring red eyes, and a row of spikes along its spine. It could run, jump, and fly at great speed.

Animal vampires

Many stories exist of animal vampires, particularly dogs. Vampire dogs were blamed for attacks on livestock in Scotland in the early 1800s, when sheep were found with bite marks to their neck.

Sightings of and attacks by El Chupacabra creatures are still being reported in Mexico, Chile, and the United States. Goats, horses, sheep, and dogs have all been found dead with bite marks.

Based on eyewitness reports, this is what El Chupacabra might look like.

57

Looking For
VAMPIRES

In some parts of eastern Europe, people tracked vampires. They were known as **dhampirs**, half-human, half-vampire. They worked on the side of humans and they had the power to see vampires.

Dhampirs ripped the sleeves off shirts and held them up like telescopes. This was how they were said to be able to see a vampire that no one else could. Having spotted one of the undead, the vampire hunter would order the creature to leave—or kill it with a silver bullet.

The end of a German vampire, when a red-hot iron is plunged into his heart until all that is left is a skeleton.

To spot a vampire when it was sleeping in its hideaway, vampire hunters searched graveyards. The hunter would pay particular attention to graves with fallen or sunken gravestones—signs that vampires might be under the ground.

If a grave was thought to contain a vampire, the body was dug up and examined by the vampire hunter for signs of vampirism, such as fresh skin, long nails, long hair, and fresh blood.

A gunshot with a silver bullet was thought to be one way to destroy a vampire.

Vampire hunter

The most famous vampire hunter was Professor Abraham Van Helsing, a doctor from Holland. He was a character created by Bram Stoker, the author of *Dracula*. In the book, Van Helsing leads the hunt for Count Dracula. The movie *Van Helsing* (2004) stars Hugh Jackman as the monster hunter.

Peter Plogojowitz, THE HUNGRY VAMPIRE

Eastern Europe seemed to be infected with vampires in the 1700s. There was one strange case—Peter Plogojowitz, an old farmer who became a deadly bloodsucker.

Peter died in 1725 in his village of Kisolava, Serbia. He was buried, but then his son claimed that his father was alive and well and had come to him, demanding food. The son did as he was told. The next night, when Peter returned, his son refused to give him food. The son was found dead the following morning.

The son gave food to the vampire, but then, when he refused, the creature killed him.

This story comes from
SERBIA

Over the next few days, several villagers died in mysterious circumstances with blood taken from their bodies. Others said they had seen Peter or dreamed that he had bitten them and sucked their blood.

Frightened villagers destroyed the vampire that had descended upon them.

Vampire madness

Stories of vampires were widespread in Germany, Austria, and Serbia in the early 1700s, leading to **vampire hysteria**. Graveyards were attacked and bodies dug up in a search for signs of the undead.

Panic set in. Soldiers were sent for, and Peter's grave was opened. Instead of finding his skeleton, they saw that his body was well preserved and his mouth was stained with blood—clear signs of vampirism. A stake was driven through Peter's heart and his body was burned until all that was left was ash.

61

How to Destroy a VAMPIRE

The only way to defeat a bloodsucker is to destroy it as completely as possible. Otherwise, it will continue infecting and killing its human and animal victims.

If a vampire was discovered, it would have to be staked to be destroyed. Stakes were made from branches cut from thorny trees, which were harmful to vampires.

In stories, the vampire was tracked down to its lair, and a long stake was hammered through its heart and into the ground. This pinned the creature to the ground and stopped the flow of blood around its body. Vampire hunters took great care not to get splashed by the blood, as it drove people crazy.

The final moments for a sleeping vampire about to be killed with a wooden stake plunged through its heart.

After the staking, the vampire's head was cut off, ideally with a gravedigger's spade. The mouth was stuffed with garlic and the head was boiled in vinegar. Then, the body was shot with a silver bullet fired by a priest.

The headless body might be buried at a crossroads and the head somewhere else. Crossroads were places of evil activity, where witches and vampires were buried. Or the vampire's head and body might be thrown onto a fire and burned to ash.

A vampire hunter's toolkit may contain a spade, vinegar, silver, and garlic. Silver was thought to be the purest of all metals, so it could defeat evil and kill vampires.

A vampire's body was buried in a separate place than the head to make sure that the vampire was completely destroyed.

Bottling a vampire

In Bulgaria, vampire hunters trapped their prey inside bottles. They forced the creature into hiding, where it stayed for days without food. The hunter put food inside a bottle to tempt the hungry vampire, and when it shrank itself down and flew into the bottle, the hunter quickly sealed it.

TIMELINE

1431-1476 Life of Vlad Dracula, known as Vlad Tepes (Vlad the Impaler). He impaled his enemies on wooden stakes.

1487 A fact book called *Malleus Maleficarum* (The Hammer of Witches) described how to destroy vampires.

1540s First reports of El Chupacabra in Arizona and New Mexico.

1720s The cases of Peter Plogojowitz and Arnold Paole, both from Serbia.

1734 The word "vampyre" came into the English language.

1810 Stories appeared in Scotland of sheep being drained of blood.

1819 The first vampire story written in English came out. It was by John Polidori and was called "The Vampyre."

1892 The case of Mercy Brown.

1897 The book *Dracula*, by Bram Stoker, was published.

1922 *Nosferatu*, a silent movie made in Germany, was released. It was based on Bram Stoker's book *Dracula*.

1976 Publication of the book *Interview with the Vampire*, the first of a series of vampire stories by Anne Rice. The film of the book was released in 1994.

1997 The TV series *Buffy the Vampire Slayer* began, starring Sarah Michelle Geller.

2004 In Romania, a man suspected of being a vampire was dug from his grave and his heart was burned to ashes.

2005 In Birmingham, England, rumors spread about the "vampire of Alum Rock," which was reported to have bitten people at night.

2005 Stephenie Meyer's book *Twilight*, the first of a series of vampire stories, became a worldwide bestseller.

The second movie in the Twilight saga was released in 2009.

GHOSTS

A WORLD OF GHOSTS

Who or what are **ghosts**? The truth is, no one knows what ghosts are, or even if they exist. However, this doesn't stop people from believing in them, and many claim to have seen ghosts. To these people, ghosts are real.

It's said that most ghosts are the **spirits** of people who have died. Instead of leaving the world of the living, they are stranded on Earth as shadowy figures that move through walls, float across the ground, and cause things to go bump in the night.

Famous ghost story

One of the most famous ghost stories ever written is *A Christmas Carol*, by Charles Dickens. The story, which came out in 1843, is about three ghosts that visit Ebenezer Scrooge on Christmas Eve to teach him about love and joy at Christmastime.

Some people believe that ghosts are friendly messengers, trying to contact the living. Others think that ghosts are harmful, seeking revenge against those who wronged them in their human lives.

When Ebenezer Scrooge was visited by ghosts, his life was never the same again.

WHO'S WHO AMONG GHOSTS?

DOPPELGANGER

Doppelganger is a German word meaning "double-walker." It is the ghost of a person who is still alive and it seems to be the person's ghostly double. The double looks like the real person, except that it has a misty, see-through appearance.

A doppelganger is thought to be a sign of bad luck that means the living person is about to die.

AND THE REST...

APPARITION, SPOOK, OR PHANTOM

The common words for a ghost, something that appears out of nowhere.

POLTERGEIST

A ghost that is invisible. It draws attention to itself by throwing things and by making banging noises. *Poltergeist* is German for "noisy ghost."

ANIMAL GHOSTS

Just like people, the spirits of some dead animals are thought to remain behind as ghosts.

The GHOSTS AT THE PALACE

When English tourists Charlotte Moberly and Eleanor Jourdain visited Versailles, France, they believed they had slipped back in time. Instead of being in the year 1901, the women felt they were in 1789 and were surrounded by ghosts from the past.

After visiting the Palace of Versailles, the ladies had walked to the nearby Petit Trianon—a grand house that once belonged to Queen Marie Antoinette. They entered the garden, and that's when the **time slip** happened.

Something felt strange, as if the world was suddenly different. The air was still and heavy. They saw gardeners at work, a young woman sketching, and a man running. Everyone was dressed in unfamiliar clothes—the clothes worn by people from long ago.

This story comes from
FRANCE

After a few minutes, the heavy feeling vanished—and so did the strange figures. Charlotte and Eleanor were convinced they had seen ghosts of the people who had once lived at Versailles and the woman seen sketching was none other than Marie Antoinette.

Charlotte and Eleanor could hardly believe their eyes—was it really the ghost of Queen Marie Antoinette?

Marie Antoinette

Marie Antoinette was born in Austria in 1755. She became Queen of France in 1774, when her husband was crowned King Louis XVI. She was unpopular with the people of France and was executed during the French Revolution in 1793.

The Causes of
GHOSTS

If ghosts really do exist, then something must cause them — but what? There are lots of ideas about the causes of ghosts, each trying to explain the mystery.

RESTLESS SPIRITS

Ghosts are the souls or spirits of dead people. Instead of leaving this world after death, the spirit stays behind, trapped and restless. It could be because it refuses to accept the death of its human body, wants to stay close to a loved one, or needs to get revenge for something bad that has happened during the person's life.

The human body has died, and in its place remains the restless spirit of a ghost.

An old house might act like a ghost trap, with a ghost always appearing at the same time every day.

Perhaps ghosts can be explained as out-of-body experiences, or OBEs. A person's spirit leaves the body while he or she is still alive, then travels to another place where it might be seen as a "ghost." The spirit returns to the body when its travels are over.

CYCLICAL GHOSTS

Eyewitnesses claim that some ghosts haunt particular places, often at set times. For example, an old house might have an apparition that appears in the same room and at the same time every day. These are so-called **cyclical ghosts**. They go around in cycles, repeating the same things.

DREAMS AND THOUGHT FORMS

Ghosts are usually seen at night, so perhaps they are no more than dreams. Another idea is that they are "thought forms," created simply by thinking about them—the result of a person's vivid imagination.

Some people believe that a ghost can be made to appear simply by the power of a person's imagination.

The Most Haunted House IN ENGLAND

Borley Rectory was doomed from the day it was built in 1863 on the site of an old monastery where a nun was said to have been buried alive. A ghost hunter claimed that it was the most haunted house in England.

Reverend Henry Bull and his family moved into their new home and, to their horror, found they were not alone. They heard footsteps, knocking, and sobbing noises and saw the shadowy figure of a nun gliding across the garden.

Reverend Bull watched as the ghost of a nun crossed the garden.

This story comes from ENGLAND

When Harry Price found the skull fragment, he was certain he had solved the mystery of Borley Rectory.

Haunted castle

Ghosts are often linked with castles. One of the world's most haunted castles is in Scotland, at Glamis. It is the haunt of the ghost of Janet Douglas, who was burned at the stake in 1537. Her ghost is said to appear over the castle clock tower, glowing orange, as if it is on fire.

The Bull family moved away in 1927 and the Smith family moved in. They also heard footsteps and sobbing, and a poltergeist threw objects across the rooms. They soon left the rectory.

Next came the Foysters, and there were more scares than ever. Writing appeared on walls, and Mrs. Foyster was slapped by an invisible hand.

Harry Price, a famous ghost hunter, contacted the spirit of a dead nun, who told him the house would burn down and the bones of a nun would be found in the ruins. In 1939, Borley Rectory burned to the ground, and when Price dug under the cellar floor, he found part of a human skull.

73

POLTERGEISTS
the Noisy Ghosts

If an object suddenly flew across the room, you might believe a poltergeist was to blame. These are invisible ghosts who make their presence known by moving objects and making noises.

WHAT IS A POLTERGEIST?

Unlike ghosts that can be seen, which might be the spirits of dead people, poltergeists are thought to be a type of energy. Whatever this energy is, it seems to be attracted to a particular person, often a teenage girl.

If objects suddenly start to move around on their own, it might be the work of a poltergeist.

Out of thin air

An object that appears out of thin air, or seems to move through solid matter, is called an apport. Most are small objects, such as items of jewelry, but larger objects, such as books, are also said to have appeared from nowhere.

STRANGE HAPPENINGS

Suddenly, and without any warning, strange things happen around the teenage girl. Earthenware is thrown across the room and smashed to pieces, objects float in the air, doors and windows open and close on their own, lights switch on and off, and things just vanish and are nowhere to be found.

NOISY SPIRITS

There's more to poltergeists than just being mischievous spirits. When all is quiet, they disturb the peace with sudden, loud bangs, tapping and scratching on walls, and rattling windows. Footsteps thud loudly across the room, bad smells fill the air, and small fires break out.

Unexplained fires, especially small ones, have been blamed on poltergeists.

The Baltimore POLTERGEIST

For three weeks in 1960, a house in Baltimore
was disturbed by strange goings-on.
Was it a poltergeist or just a faulty boiler?

It started when the Jones family was having their
evening meal. Suddenly, a vase exploded into
tiny pieces, and then another, and
another, until fifteen lay broken
on the floor.

Ted seemed to be at the
center of the poltergeist
activity—but why?

Over the next few days, pictures popped off their hooks and crashed to the ground, and a sugar bowl floated through the air, then spilled sugar onto a table.

A ghost hunter visited the family. He noticed that seventeen-year-old Ted's passion for writing was ignored. So Ted's feelings of frustration built up inside him until they turned into an energy force—a force that had the power to move objects. This, said the ghost hunter, accounted for the poltergeist activity.

A ghost hunter thought Ted could make objects move simply by thinking about them.

Mind control — fact or fiction?

The power to move objects by thought alone is called **psychokinesis**, or PK. Many people have said they can do this, especially those who claim they can make contact with spirits. Some people think it's no more than stage magic, designed to trick people.

A plumber said it was because air pressure had built up inside the house from the boiler. He told the family to open the windows so that the pressure inside the house would be the same as outside. They did as they were told, and the weird things stopped. In the Jones' minds, the plumber had solved the mystery.

This story comes from
Maryland

77

TALKING TO GHOSTS

If ghosts are real, perhaps it's because they want to make contact with the living. This idea has been around for thousands of years, and many people claim to have talked to them.

TALKING TO SPIRITS

In tribal communities, people with this gift are shamans, medicine men, and wise women. Elsewhere they are known as **psychics**, mystics, and, most of all, **mediums**. Ghost talkers usually enter into trances to contact the spirit world. They act as go-betweens, linking the world of the living with the world of the dead.

Shamans are believed to have the power to talk to the dead.

The Ouija board

At a séance, a medium might use a Ouija (say: we-ja) board. The letters of the alphabet are printed on the board, and a pointer rests on top of it. A question is asked, and if a spirit answers it, the pointer moves from letter to letter, spelling out the spirit's reply.

A photograph from the 1920s showing people taking part in a séance.

SPIRIT MEETINGS

For many people, the idea of contacting the spirit of a loved one is irresistible. It's a chance to ask questions and, hopefully, receive answers. Mediums hold a meeting to contact the spirits called a **séance**. People can ask questions, and the medium passes on the spirits' answers.

FAKES

Many mediums have been found out to be fakes. They change the sound of their voices and only pretend to be speaking to spirits. They make up answers that people want to hear.

The Table-tapping SISTERS

Maggie and Kate Fox from the town of Hydesville said they could talk to spirits. People flocked to their house, eager to contact their loved ones who had died. The year was 1848.

It all began when Maggie, aged 15, and Kate, aged 12, discovered that when they clapped their hands, a rapping noise answered back. It was as if the girls were being used as a channel to reach into the spirit world.

The girls' claps and the ghostly raps were used to spell out letters, which built up into words and sentences. Newspapers reported on these events, and the Fox sisters became well known. They gave public performances, where strange rapping noises were accompanied by flying objects and floating tables.

Maggie and Kate Fox caused a sensation when they said they could contact the spirit world.

The sisters carried on with their acts of spiritualism for many years. Then, in 1888, Maggie and Kate confessed that they had been pretending all along. They had made the rapping noises by cracking the joints of their toes.

Sir Arthur Conan Doyle

Arthur Conan Doyle (1859–1930) is best known as the writer of the Sherlock Holmes detective stories. He was also a big fan of spiritualism and wrote several books about the subject.

This story comes from
New York

Ghosts on CAMERA

Is it possible to prove that ghosts exist? Ghost hunters think it is. They started taking cameras and other recording equipment to haunted places and have recorded some truly unusual images.

TAKING PHOTOGRAPHS

For many people, photographs of ghosts are fake. Some might have been made on purpose to fool people. Others might be tricks of the light or shadows. Today, cameras are everywhere, which can only mean there's a greater chance of photographing something unusual—something that might just prove the existence of ghosts.

A group of ghost hunters from Rhode Island, called the Valley Rangers Paranormal Investigators, bang on a door at a cemetery to provoke the ghosts that dwell there.

RAYNHAM HALL

One of the most famous ghost photographs of all time was taken by chance. It happened in 1936, when magazine photographers took pictures inside Raynham Hall, a country house in Norfolk, England.

A photograph of the main staircase showed the ghostly figure of a woman in a wedding dress. The house is said to be haunted by Lady Dorothy Townshend, who once lived there. Her ghost, known as the Brown Lady, has been seen many times.

The Brown Lady ghost, photographed at Raynham Hall in 1936.

Raynham Hall is a country house in Norfolk, England. Its famous ghost might be of Lady Dorothy Townshend, who lived there in the early 1700s.

Ghost on the phone

The phone rings, and the voice on the other end is from someone who has died. The line is crackly, as if the ghostly voice is calling from far away. Soon, the voice fades, until all that is left on the line is the empty sound of silence.

HOUSE
OF HORRORS

In December 1975, George and Kathleen Lutz moved into their new house in Amityville. The year before, a family had been murdered there, and when the house was put up for sale, no one wanted it—except the Lutzes.

Within a month of moving in, the Lutzes fled the house. They said it was filled with a bad smell, slime oozed from the walls, and there were swarms of flies. Doors slammed, and footprints from an unknown creature were found in the snow. Mrs. Lutz claimed she was grabbed by unseen hands, and one night she said she floated up from her bed and turned into a wrinkled old lady.

The Lutzes told their story to a writer, and his book, *The Amityville Horror: A True Story*, became a bestseller and was made into a successful movie. The problem was, it was just that—a story.

Haunted prison

The island of Alcatraz, in San Francisco Bay, was home to a famous prison. Alcatraz closed in 1963 and is now visited by tourists. Some have said they felt they were being watched and could hear footsteps and shouting. Others claim to have seen the ghosts of prisoners passing through the walls, as if trying to escape.

When investigators looked into the story, they were certain the whole thing was a **hoax**. For example, no snow had fallen on the night the Lutzes said they found the footprints. The whole thing had been made up by the Lutzes.

It might look like a scene from a horror movie, but the Lutzes said that slime covered the walls of their house.

GHOSTLY LIGHTS

According to ghost hunters, ghosts don't need to appear in human shape. Balls of light known as **orbs** can be detected only by cameras that show infrared images. The light floats through the air in straight lines, as if a person is walking along.

Only after this photograph was taken did people see the bright light next to the man. The question is, what is it?

TRICK OF THE EYE

Orbs have been photographed and filmed many times, and different ideas exist to explain them. For people who do not believe in ghosts, orbs are simply specks of dust, grains of pollen, or water droplets reflected back into the lens of the camera.

ENERGY FORMS

However, for believers in ghosts, orbs are signs of something else. These people believe that orbs are forms of pure energy that are released when a person dies. The spirits of the dead use orbs to show that they are still here among the living.

Another idea says that orbs are bundles of energy from events that happened in the past, trapped in the atmosphere. The bigger the event was, the more energy would have been released.

Orbs of light, photographed over the prehistoric Avebury stones in Wiltshire, England.

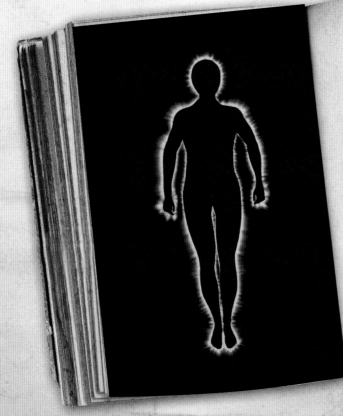

Glow in the dark

There's said to be a glowing light around the body of every living person. This was discovered in the 1930s by Russian professor Semyan Kirlian. He took photographs that showed sparks of light coming from people's bodies.

87

The Black Cat of KILLAKEE

Over the centuries, cats have been linked to mysterious happenings. When a cat arches its back and hisses, it's because it has seen a ghost. As for the Black Cat of Killakee, it was a ghost itself.

At long last, the old house in the village of Killakee, Ireland, was being repaired. It had stood empty for many years, and locals said that it was haunted by the ghost of a giant cat.

There were rumors that the old house at Killakee was haunted—but this didn't faze the builders.

One day in 1968, the door to the house was found open, and when a workman went inside he found a ghostly black cat as big as a dog staring at him through blood-red eyes.

The cat was bigger than a normal cat, and its eyes were the color of blood.

Long-lost cats

The dried-out mummified bodies of cats are sometimes found inside old buildings in Europe. It was believed that cats brought good luck, so builders hid cats behind walls and under floorboards, thinking they would protect the house.

This was just the start. Over the coming weeks, the house echoed to the sound of knocks and bangs, vases were smashed, and pictures fell from the walls, as if a poltergeist was present. It was all too much for Margaret O'Brien, the owner, who asked a priest to rid the house of the harmful spirit. The priest did this and all was well.

Hunting For GHOSTS

Science became involved with ghost hunting when the first photographs of ghostly shapes were taken. Today's ghost hunters set camcorders running, equipped with lenses that can see in the dark.

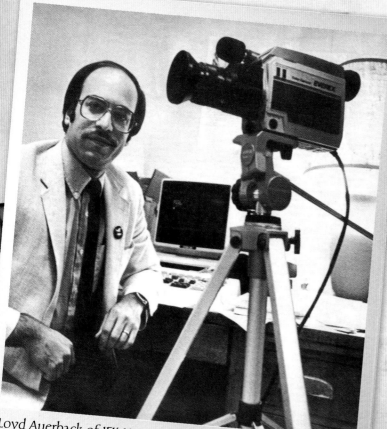

Loyd Auerback of JFK University, California, conducts field investigations of paranormal activity, using photographic equipment.

INVESTIGATING THE SCENE

Other devices look for sudden drops in the temperature, since it's thought this indicates a ghostly presence. Eyewitnesses are interviewed, facts are checked and double-checked, and a description slowly emerges. It's like police work, investigating the scene of a crime.

FINDING AN EXPLANATION

When ghost hunters begin looking into a new case, they know they might find nothing unusual. Perhaps they find that a knocking noise can be explained by a loose pipe. A ghost photograph might turn out to be the result of a faulty camera.

It's been calculated that 98 percent of all ghost stories can be given everyday explanations. That leaves 2 percent that can't be explained. It's these rare cases that might just prove that ghosts really do exist.

An investigator measures the presence of electricity in the ground of a cemetery. They believe that this might show paranormal activity.

Harry Price, Ghost Hunter

Harry Price (1881–1948) was a famous ghost hunter from England. In the 1920s, he started using scientific methods to look for ghosts. He set up a laboratory where he carried out experiments. Price also investigated haunted places and wrote several books about his findings.

TIMELINE

1537 Janet Douglas was burned at the stake. Her ghost is said to haunt Glamis Castle, Scotland, and is known as the Grey Lady.

1817 A poltergeist known as the Bell Witch pestered the Bell family in Adams, Tennessee for four years.

1843 The ghost story *A Christmas Carol*, by Charles Dickens, was published.

1848 Maggie and Kate Fox, of Hydesville, claimed they could communicate with the spirit world.

1863 Borley Rectory was built and became notorious as the most haunted house in England. It was destroyed by fire in 1939.

1901 Charlotte Moberly and Eleanor Jourdain believed they had seen the ghost of Queen Marie Antoinette at Versailles, France.

1920s Harry Price began his work as a ghost hunter in England.

1936 The Brown Lady photograph was taken at Raynham Hall, Norfolk, England. It is one of the most famous ghost photographs ever taken.

1939 *The Friendly Ghost*, a book for children, was published. It featured a ghost called Casper.

1975 George and Kathleen Lutz claimed their house in Amityville was haunted. A book and movie about the events were made.

1984 The movie *Ghostbusters* was released.

Ghostbusters was about a team of ghost catchers in New York City.

2008 A photograph taken at Tantallon Castle, Scotland, seems to show a figure of a woman in Tudor clothes.

BILL MURRAY   DAN AYKROYD
SIGOURNEY WEAVER
GH\STBUSTERS

GLOSSARY

CANNIBAL
A person who eats the flesh of other humans. Also, an animal that feeds on others of its own kind.

CYCLICAL GHOST
A type of ghost that appears in the same place again and again.

DHAMPIR
A hybrid creature thought to be part vampire, part human. Dhampirs, who came from eastern Europe, were good at detecting vampires.

DOPPELGANGER
A type of ghost. It means "double-walker" and is the ghostly double of a person who is still alive.

FOLK STORIES
Traditional stories told in particular regions of the world. They began as spoken word stories and may have been very old by the time they were written down for the first time.

GHOST
The image of a person, an animal, or a thing such as a ship that is not really there.

HOAX
Something that is made up on purpose and is meant to make people believe it is real.

INVOLUNTARY WEREWOLF
A person who does not want to become a werewolf, but when a werewolf scratches or bites the person, he or she is changed into one.

LYCANTHROPE
Another word for a werewolf. It comes from two Greek words— *lykos* meaning "wolf," and *anthropos* meaning "human."

MEDIUM
A person who claims he or she can contact the dead.

MUSKET
A gun with a long barrel that fires a ball of lead.

ORB
A ball of light that can only be seen with a camera and which is claimed to be a form of ghostly energy.

PENTAGRAM
A star with five points, thought to have magical powers.

POLTERGEIST
A type of ghost. It moves objects, causes fires, and makes noises.

PSYCHIC
A person who claims he or she can read minds and perform other mysterious actions.

GLOSSARY

PSYCHOKINESIS
The power to make an object move just by thinking about it.

SÉANCE
A meeting at which people work with a medium to contact the dead.

SHAPE-SHIFT
The ability of a vampire or werewolf to change its shape from one thing to another. A vampire can change into a bat or mist, whereas a werewolf can change into its wolflike form, and then back again.

SPIRIT
Another word for a ghost. It can also mean a person's soul.

STAKE
A wooden stick with a pointed end, used to kill a vampire by stabbing it through its heart.

TIME SLIP
The feeling that time has somehow changed from the present day to the past.

TRANSFORMATION
The process of changing a human into a vampire.

TRANSYLVANIA
A mountainous region of Romania, southeast Europe, which is the setting for Bram Stoker's vampire novel about Count Dracula.

TURNING
Another word for transformation. A person who becomes a vampire has been "turned" into one of the undead.

UNDEAD
A creature, such as a vampire, that lives in two worlds—the world of the living and the world of the dead.

UNHALLOWED
Unholy ground that is linked with evil and harmful forces.

VAMPIRE HYSTERIA
When many people in a community panic because they think they are threatened by one or more vampires.

VOLUNTARY WEREWOLF
A person who wants to become a werewolf.

WOLF BELT
A belt of wolfskin worn around the waist, which has the power to transform a person into a werewolf.

INDEX